cl🍀verleaf books™

Nature's Patterns

What Is It Made Of?
Noticing Types of Materials

Martha E. H. Rustad

illustrated by Christine M. Schneider

M MILLBROOK PRESS · MINNEAPOLIS

For Devon and Ayden,
from Auntie Martha —M.E.H.R.

For Dad —C.M.S.

Millbrook Press
A division of Lerner Publishing Group, Inc.
241 First Avenue North
Minneapolis, MN 55401 USA

For reading levels and more information, look up this title at
www.lernerbooks.com.

Main body text set in Slappy Inline 18/28.
Typeface provided by T26.

Library of Congress Cataloging-in-Publication Data

Rustad, Martha E. H. (Martha Elizabeth Hillman), 1975– author.
    What is it made of? : noticing types of materials / by
 Martha E. H. Rustad.
       pages   cm. — (Cloverleaf books. Nature's patterns)
    Summary: "Introduction to the properties of materials."--
 Provided by publisher.
    Audience: Ages 5–8.
    Audience: K to grade 3.
    Includes bibliographical references and index.
    ISBN 978-1-4677-8561-7 (lb : alk. paper)
    ISBN 978-1-4677-8607-2 (pb : alk. paper)
    ISBN 978-1-4677-8608-9 (EB pdf)
    1. Materials science--Juvenile literature. 2. Matter—
 Properties—Juvenile literature. I. Title.
 TA403.2.R87 2015
 620.1'1--dc23   2014041004

Manufactured in the United States of America
1 – BP – 7/15/15

TABLE OF CONTENTS

Chapter One
The Guessing Game

We are playing a game today! Our teacher, Ms. Sampson, puts something in a bag. Then Thea puts in her hand and tells what it feels like. **Our job is to guess what it is!**

"It feels round and hard," says Thea.

"A bouncy ball!" guesses Micah.

"No, it's a flat circle," Thea says.

"And it's a little bumpy."

Jae guesses a quarter. **She's right!**

Quarters are made from a mixture of two metals, copper and nickel. Before 1965, they were made from silver and copper.

5

We talk about how **coins are made from metal** and bouncy balls are made from rubber.

Our teacher asks, "Would it work to make a coin from rubber?"

"A bouncy coin?" asks Jorge. **"No way!"**

materials

Ms. Sampson tells us that we are starting a new project. We are going to learn about materials.

"What are materials?" Izzy asks.

"Materials are what we use to make things," Ms. Sampson says.

Most metals come from rock in the ground. Natural rubber comes from rubber trees. But many rubber objects are made with human-made rubber.

7

Chapter Two
What Is It Made Of?

To start our project, Ms. Sampson tells us to look around our classroom.

"What types of materials do you see?" she asks.

"Our windows are made of glass," Amal says.

"This chair is made of wood," Jake says.

Olivia says, "My shirt is made of fabric."

- Metal
- Rubber
- Wood
- Glass
- Plastic
- Fabric
- Rock

Ms. Sampson

Ms. Sampson asks, "Would it work to make a window out of wood? Or a shirt out of glass?"

Everyone laughs. Amal shakes his head. "**That would be silly.**"

"Why?" our teacher wonders.

"Because windows have to be clear!" Olivia answers.

Jake says, "And a shirt has to be soft!"

"**Good thinking**," Ms. Sampson says. "People choose different materials for different purposes."

Next, Ms. Sampson puts different materials on a table. "Let's make a list of words that describe these materials," she says.

First, we talk about **how the materials feel.**

"This spoon is hard and smooth," Micah says.

Thea says, "This pile of sand feels soft and cool."

"This eraser is bendy," Olivia says.
Then we talk about **how they look.**
"These coins are shiny," Izzy says.
Jorge says, "This tree bark looks dull and brown."
"Those glasses look clear," says Amal.

- Hard or Soft
- Bendy or Stiff
  Smooth or Rough
  Light or Heavy
  Colors
  Clear or Not
  Shiny or Dull

Sand is made of tiny pieces of hard rock. But it feels soft because wind and water have worn down the pieces and made them smooth.

Chapter Three

Treasure Hunt

We are going on a treasure hunt around the school! We're searching for different kinds of materials and recording how they look and feel. We keep track on charts we made.

Ms. Sampson says, "Let's look for objects made of wood."

We see chairs and desks.

We spot the gym floor and doors.

We find craft sticks and pencils.

Next, we look for items made of metal.
We find paper clips and coins.
We see lockers and doorknobs.
We spot faucets and earrings.

16

"Great finds!" says Ms. Sampson.

"Metal is a useful material for making many objects." **We're super treasure hunters!** But our hunt isn't over. We search for rock, plastic, glass, and other materials.

Back in our classroom, Ms. Sampson tells us to look at our charts.

"Do you see any patterns?" she asks. She reminds us that a pattern is something that happens again and again.

"Both wood and metal are hard," Izzy says. "Is that a pattern?"

	Hard or Soft	Bendy or Stiff	Smooth or Rough	Light or Heavy	Colors	Clear or Not	
Metal	hard	stiff	smooth	both	gold, silver, copper, and more	not clear	
Rubber	soft	bendy	smooth	light	pink, blue, yellow, and many more	not clear	
Wood	hard	stiff	rough	light	mostly brown	not clear	
Glass	hard	stiff	smooth				
Plastic	hard and soft	both	smooth	light	many colors	both	
Fabric	soft	bendy	rough or smooth	light	many colors	not clear	
Rock	hard	stiff	smooth	heavy	grey, brown, black, and more	not clear	

"**Yes!**" says Ms. Sampson. "What else?"

"The glass windows and my plastic pencil box are both clear," Jake says.

Jae says, "Rubber bands and my shirt are both stretchy and bendy."

Some materials change when the temperature goes up or down. Metal softens when it is heated. So does glass. Then people or machines can form them into different shapes.

We learned about a lot of materials.

Time to make a sculpture in art class! Ms. Sampson wonders what materials we will use.

Jae uses wood craft sticks.
Izzy picks shiny metal foil.
Micah finds plastic eyes.
Jorge cuts pieces of fabric.
Sticky glue holds it all together!

Guessing Game

See if your friends or family can guess what's in a guessing bag!

What You Need

a paper or cloth bag

a variety of objects made from different materials, such as wooden clothespins, metal paper clips, paper cups, cotton balls, balloons, or glass marbles

1) Ask everyone to close both eyes while you put one object in the guessing bag.

2) Choose one friend or family member to feel what's in the bag. Ask that person to describe the item to the rest of the group.

3) Have the group guess what the object is and what material it's made from.

4) After everyone is done guessing, have the person take the object out of the bag so the group can see it.

5) Take turns describing and guessing what different objects are in the bag.

GLOSSARY

copper: a type of metal that is orange in color

materials: substances people use to make things

metal: a hard material that mostly comes from rock in the ground

nickel: a type of metal that looks silver in color

patterns: things that are repeated again and again

quarter: a US coin worth twenty-five cents

recording: writing something down

rubber: a bendy, stretchy material

BOOKS

Boothroyd, Jennifer. *How Big? How Heavy? How Dense? A Look at Matter*. Minneapolis: Lerner Publications, 2011. Learn about the properties of different materials.

Boothroyd, Jennifer. *Many Kinds of Matter: A Look at Solids, Liquids, and Gases.* Minneapolis: Lerner Publications, 2011. Learn about how different temperatures affect different materials.

Fletcher, Sheila. *Is It Flexible or Rigid?* New York: Crabtree, 2012. Learn about patterns in materials that are bendy or stiff.

Mason, Helen. *Is It Hard or Soft?* New York: Crabtree, 2014. Read about materials that are hard and soft, and the ways people use them.

WEBSITES

Sorting and Using Materials
http://www.bbc.co.uk/schools/scienceclips/ages/5_6/sorting_using_mate.shtml
Test the properties of different materials.

States of Matter
http://www.neok12.com/States-of-Matter.htm
Play games, watch videos, and take quizzes about what happens to different materials in different temperatures.

LERNER ᴇ SOURCE™
Expand learning beyond the printed book. Download free, complementary educational resources for this book from our website, www.lerneresource.com.